THE ISLANDS OF IRELAND

Tory Island

Owey Island
Aranmore Island

Rathlin Island

Lough Arrow

Clare
Island

Inishturk

Inishbofin
Inishark

Friar Island

Caher Island

Mayflies Islands

Lough Corrib

Inis Meáin

Great Blasket
Island

Skellig
Islands

Dursey   Bere
Island Island

THE ISLANDS OF IRELAND

Nutan

Thames & Hudson

Translated from the French by Nutan and Joe Aston

First published in hardcover in the United States of America in 2005 by
Thames & Hudson Inc., 500 Fifth Avenue, New York, New York 10110

thamesandhudsonusa.com

ISBN-13: 978-0-500-51258-6
ISBN-10: 0-500-51258-2

Library of Congress Catalog Number: 2005923408

Printed and bound in China

EUROPEAN UNION
STRUCTURAL FUNDS

NATIONAL DEVELOPMENT PLAN

The author would like to thank Comhdháil Oileáin na hEireann's
National Rural Development Programme, which is financed by the
Irish Government under the National Development Plan 2000–06
and by European Union Structural Funds.

Contents

Nutan on board the Anna M.

A Voyage through Time

On one side, the Irish Sea, on the other, the Atlantic. Our feet in myriad marshes, rivers and lakes, capped with mist, hammered by rain; truly we live in the water.

As schoolchildren, we learn from childhood that islands are pieces of land surrounded by water. What's more, in this small country, they are usually visible from the coast, and hence more seductive; so close, yet out of reach. This continual difficulty of access makes the object more fascinating. In the interior of the country, the great lakes themselves also cradle hundreds of islands. Lough Corrib alone has 365, one for each day of the year. They are mystical witnesses to our past and to a more serene way of life. One hundred years ago there were 100 inhabited islands; now there are about 30.

Some modernize, others empty. Many children of the islands, expatriated out of necessity to America, Australia or any of the four corners of the globe, return at the end of their lives to the rock where they were born. They build new houses or modernize the cottage of their birth. Some never leave and remain the guardians of a precious civilization.

Nowadays tourists have become a major support for the survival of these little communities, who do not have the luxury of choice. Indeed, there are others who come as well: writers, attracted by the silence and raw nature; painters, drawn by the play of light and the strong primary forms; and the other blow-ins who seem to come by chance. I think myself that they all come primarily to search for their own inner self.

As a photographer and a fisherman, I was naturally attracted to the place. It was not surpising that my fascination with the rough, open-air life of sea and country people should lead me to become a fisherman in Killybegs, Ireland's largest fishing port.

Hidden at the bottom of the northwest coast in Donegal, the Killybegs of the 1970s was very different to today's port. 'High tech' had yet to happen and the work was done by hand or with the help of fairly primitive equipment. Fishing technology, which today works with such fearsome efficiency, was still in its infancy. The seas were full of fish. The fishermen, though hard-working, skilled and persevering, still had time to sit on a creel to savour their hard and honest way of life, to wonder, furtively, at its simple quality and the beauty of their environment.

A little anecdote: on a cutout cartoon strip, stuck to the back of the toilet door in a dockside pub, a fisherman sits on a creel puffing on his pipe and admiring the clouds of blue smoke emanating from it. An American businessman greets him as he passes, and demands to know what he's doing. 'But can't you see? I've come in from fishing and I'm resting a little before I go fixing my lobster pots!'

The American retorts that if he put in a little more effort he could catch more and make more money. Then, if he managed things properly, he could buy a bigger boat, catch even more fish, and make enough money so that he could afford to employ someone else to take the boat out, and then he would be able to sit back and rest....

'Funny,' replies the fisherman, 'can't you see that's what I'm already doing?'

This story struck me at the time, and, indeed, perhaps it was the seed that, quietly growing in me over the years, finally resulted in this book on the islands of the west coast of Ireland. They are the last bastions of an ancient civilization, protected by inhospitable seas and

Alice Guerraz gripping the wheel.

Joe Aston, skipper of the Anna M.

a changeable climate, which prevent it from crumbling too quickly before the onslaught of the 'Celtic Tiger'. While in contemporary Ireland, caught up in vertiginous economic development, it is hard to find that majestic old quality of life, in most of the islands that I have visited it remains intact...although it is frequently eroded and sometimes both physically and spiritually abandoned. I had hoped to find time and money to visit every island. Unfortunately, I could hardly manage to reach twenty. In order to show their differences, though they are limited enough as they do form a geographical unit, I tried to portray human or geophysical aspects as diverse and distinct as possible.

I was always up against the fact that they are only bits of rock, continuously assaulted by waves that may vary in their cruelty, but not in their persistence. The inhabitants or the habitat of one or another may have their unique characteristics, but they are all cast in the same mould: ancient, graven, isolated among ever-present granite and swell. It was with my old friend and fishing skipper, Joe Aston, aboard his majestic schooner, *Anna M*, that I did most of the voyaging. I dedicate this book to to this faithful servant, to the Atlantic spray, sometimes kindly but mostly not, to all the people I have met in the course of my own personal voyage started back in the 1970s. Also to my father, who from the cradle gave me a taste for fishing and nature.... The technological novelties of our modern world need to be integrated with the ancestral traditions of these jewels of the ocean. A challenge reserved for honest jugglers. I hope they will be clever and inspired enough to preserve such rare individuality.

I would like to thank: Darren and Mary Shannon, Mick McGinley, Spoutnik, Blondie, Paul Cullen, Jeff O'Connell, Joe, Luke and James Aston, Tobias, Fergus Lyons, Mick and Pauline O'Toole, Phil and Bernard Heanue, Jack Heanue, Noel Heaney, John Concannon, Dany Kirrane, Máiread O'Reilly, Mary and Bill Heanue, Mary Sugrue, Finola O'Shucrue, Debbie Browne, Herbie, Jim and Liam McFaul, Ted Keane, Deidre O'Toole, Tarlach and Aine de Blácam, Máire Pháidín, Teach Osta Inis Meáin, Ruairi and Máirin O Coinceanainn, Dara Beag O Fátharta, Anthony Moylan, Michael D. Higgins, TD, Eamon O Cuív, TD, Minister for Community, Rural and Gaeltacht Affairs, Mairéad O'Reilly, Programmes Manager, Comhdháil Oileáin na hEireann. Naomie Rogers, Anton Meehan, Patsy Dan Rodgers, Alice Guerraz, Yasmine Lamouche, Lionel Hoebeke, Aline Gougon, Bernadette Caille, Françine Deroudille, Jean-Luc Manaud, Georges Thiry, Georges Rémy, Yellow, Bullet, Charlie O'Hara, Rosalind Neely, Charlotte Troy and Mark Lane. To those I forgot, I apologize and I thank you for all your help and for being there for me. This book is for you all.

7

FROM ISLAND TO ISLAND

Wherever the wind blows

Seven o'clock in the morning, 10 July 2004. Legs jammed under the sink, my back braced against the bulk head of the 'heads'. For the fourth time today I try in vain to pour some water in the kettle to make tea. The galley of the *Anna M* is small and anything that is not fixed flies all over the place. It's blowing hard, the sea is more than lively, and as we claw to the north of Aranmore we are shaken by some fairly nasty waves.

Fresh water, which must always be used sparingly at sea, spouts diagonally from the tap, now to the left and now to the right, and obstinately refuses to go into the required opening. Being cook on a boat is not an easy job: you need

Sunset on Cromane Island, Co. Kerry. Benoît, a French oyster farmer, brings his barge ashore. Born into a long line of oyster farmers in Brittany, he has been working the Cromane Bay for the last five years or so. Cromane is famous for the quality of its shellfish.

Exhausted after a long autumn day, I drag my tired feet to the top of a rocky hill to take a picture of Bray Head, the southwest point of Valentia Island, Co. Kerry.

a sound stomach, and must be able to improvise within
the limitations of the boat, tirelessly doing and redoing the
same old tasks. I have cooked for years on fishing boats,
and it is on the sailing boat of my old fishing skipper, Joe,
that I now find myself, at sea again.

I would go to the ends of the world with him, under
sail. He has an incredible sense of the sea, and when he
is at the helm, even if the hair stands up on our heads,
everything goes well. At least, most things do. As for Alice,
our passenger, I met her on the docks at Galway. She wanted
to go sketching on the islands and didn't have any money.

The schooner Anna M, *our
faithful servant, glides past the
Teelin rocks on its way to our
night's anchorage.*

*Seen from Cillrealig artists'
retreat, a moody morning sky
over Hog's Head, Scariff
Island and Deenish Island.*

When I suggested to her that she could come with us, she promptly accepted. Holding on to the wheel for grim death, with her arms stretched out to St Christopher, she looks quite wild. She had never set foot in a boat before. Well, she has now.

So here I am, the photographer who ordered this voyage, juggling kettle and saucepans. Joe's cooking is...pretty basic and Alice hasn't the sea legs for it yet. Life is not fair.

The contents of our pantry says a lot about the life of this boat. The box of tea bears the stamp of a shop in the Azores, the gas lighter is a gift from the fishermen's cooperative of the Cape Verde Islands, the butter and milk come from a

It is cold this October morning. Hidden behind the clouds, the sun tries, in vain, to warm up the Donegal coast near Owey Island.

pub on the Aran Islands. A can of tuna breaks loose and
hits me on the shoulder. It is two years out of date and
comes from a store at Le Palais, Belle Isle, where Joe and
I spent a while in the winter three years ago.

It's often the state of the sea that decides the day's menu.
If it's calm enough, you might try something fancy and
figure out what ingredients are available before fixing on
a definite plan. If the sea is up, everything is shaken about.
If a box of Spanish chocolate powder turns up beside some
dried sardines from God knows where, *voilà*, the menu is
decided. It's my little job to prepare it so that it's eatable.

*The wind suddenly gets up
and churns the sea into a
frothy broth. A timid sun
lights up the white horses,
as we seem to fly towards
menacing black clouds ahead.*

Emerging from the morning mist,
an old observation tower nestles
among the rocks of Carrigan Head,
north of Teelin, Co. Donegal.

As the mackerel are running on the west coast of Ireland, the menu is not very varied. Grilled or fried with onions, in curry, soup or hot pot…I have mackerel coming out of my ears.

How did the island people manage to survive with the little they had? It is a question that often comes to mind when you visit these rocks that are so bare. Apart from milk and wild birds' eggs, harvested from steep cliffs that would take the breath out of you, they had tea, flour, sugar and tobacco, provided, that is, that the sea was calm enough for them to go to the mainland in curraghs

All along the Donegal coast,
rising like old crumpled potatoes,
rocks of pink granite make a brave
stand against the constant waves
that besiege them.

(tarred sea boats) when they had the few pence in their pockets to buy them. The rest had to come from the land and the sea, according to the season and each person's skills.

It was a tough, harsh life, that wore the hands but kept the eyes clear. In India long ago I heard Bhagwan Shree Rajneesh state: 'Choice is a prison'. If you have two pairs of shoes, which one do you put on? At least on the islands they weren't too troubled by such problems. Shoes or no shoes, you made the best of it.

Black shags sun themselves at the bottom of the cliffs on Inishnabro, one of the islands of the archipelago of the Blasket islands, Co. Kerry.

I recall an anecdote that a friend told me twenty years ago. In the early years of the twentieth century, little Island Eddy in Galway Bay boasted one hundred or so inhabitants. When I knew them, in the 1970s, Mary and John Bermingham were the last two survivors. They didn't speak to each other and lived in two different houses. One day, Mary fell ill and was taken to hospital. After a while she came back to her island, but she died there a few days later. John left the island shortly after, going to live in a nearby village, and saying that he couldn't manage living on his own. What are you to make of human nature?

It is at the bottom of the famous Bunglass cliffs, north of Teelin, Co. Donegal, that you will find the giant's chair and table. I can see him from here enjoying a fry of puffin eggs and crabmeat, his toes wriggling in delight among the seaweed....

*Sailing close to Cruit rocks, the
sun lights up wild waves that
seem to crash for my pleasure
in elegant pearly sprays.*

Today life on the islands has changed a lot. Most
of the houses are crowned with television aerials or
satellite dishes. There are regular connections by boat,
sometimes even by air, on some of them. One can come
and go. The Government has set up cooperatives that
help to improve the infrastructure and the quality
of life. Materially, life has become much easier there.
By contrast, those aerials and satellite dishes are not
necessarily positive signs of progress. They are, for me,
like funnels by which much that is dubious penetrates
the islands.

*Rathlin O'Beirne's lighthouse
seems a friendly place in the
sunlight on our horizon. Its
treacherous currents and dangerous rocks are famous for the
many lives they have claimed
among seagoing folk.*

For centuries, Horse Island, off Ballinskelligs, Co. Kerry, supported two families: the MacGearailts and the de Barras. They left it after one too many vicious storms in November 1959. The only sur- viving white-washed cottage was bought by an English family who uses it as a holiday house.

RATHLIN ISLAND
Puffin island

The island lies about 9 kilometres (6 miles) off Ballycastle in northeast Ireland and 25 kilometres (16 miles) from the Mull of Kintyre in Scotland. Because it is so close, it has often been at the centre of many an argument over ownership. The dispute was finally settled in 1617 by a simple test: if a snake could survive on the island, it would be taken as being part of the mainland. If it died, then Ireland would own the island. Storms must have killed the snake! Rathlin is Irish.

Probably the first island to become inhabited around 6,000 BC, it has had a tumultuous history, surviving three massacres and the terrible famine of 1846. Local stories tell of 300 islanders leaving on the same day, and the dogs they had abandoned howling after them from the cliffs.

Rathlin is surrounded by some forty recorded shipwrecks, treacherous currents and mountainous spring tides. Three lighthouses stand, nestled amongst dramatic cliffs of up to 143 metres (470 feet), above caves and underwater cliffs. The west lighthouse is the most impressive. It required feats of engineering to build a provisional pier, a steep cable tramway from the pier to the cliff top and a 3 kilometre (2 mile) stretch of road so that the rocks of Kebble could be hacked away to lay the foundations for the lighthouse. It took five years of hard and dangerous labour before the light was eventually switched on.

There are many legends associated with the island, including the most famous one of the Enchanted Island that appears from the sea once every seven years.

Rathlin gave shelter to numerous famous figures. The most famous was Robert the Bruce, who hid there after being defeated by the English at Perth in 1306. While hidden in a cave in Rathlin, he drew inspiration from a spider, which tried seven times to bridge the gap between two rocks. Infused with fresh courage, Robert the Bruce then made a further attempt at the crown, eventually succeeding at the battle of Bannockburn in 1314. Rathlin's most recent claim to fame is when Richard Branson's hot-air balloon crashed into the sea off Bull Point and was rescued by a local fishing boat.

There are many legends associated with the island, including the most famous one of the Enchanted Island that appears from the sea once every seven years. If you lift a stone from under your feet and throw it on to the island, then it will never disappear again.

Liam McFaul, RSPB warden, keeps a close watch on his winged charges.

It is also from Rathlin that Guglielmo Marconi successfully transmitted the first commercial radio signals across water in 1898. The island has always been famous for its smuggling: poteen (illicit spirit), rum, brandy, tobacco and...lace.

Today tourism and the largest colony of Atlantic puffins in Europe drive Rathlin's fragile economy. Easily identifiable by their orange bills and webbed feet, the pigeon-sized puffins are friendly and quite comical-looking seabirds that nest underground. From April to August it is their breeding season on Rathlin.... They use their sharp toes to scratch out burrows where the female will lay a single egg that is incubated in turn by both parents for about forty days. The off-duty parent will go fishing for capelin and sand eels, their favourite food, while the egg is being hatched.

Built for swimming rather than for flying, they can use their wings for propulsion and their webbed feet for manoeuvring when underwater. On land, puffins are agile and can stand and walk nimbly on their toes. It is in the air that the dignified puffin becomes a bit awkward. To get airborne, they must run along the water surface for a long way before take-off. They feed in flocks and the young are fed in the nest for up to two months. Once fledged, they remain on the open sea and will not come back to their native cliffs before the second or third year.

The RSPB (Royal Society for the Protection of Birds) has installed a spectacular viewing platform overlooking two great towers of basalt rocks that are home to a very noisy bird population. From there, you can watch thousands of guillemots, kittiwakes, gulls and gannets twirl around you.... Armed with binoculars and tripods, hundreds of bird-watchers flock to the cliff each year and contribute some welcome cash to the local economy. Liam McFaul, the RSPB warden, is responsible for looking after the puffins. It is not so long since puffins' eggs and the puffins themselves were on the daily menu.

PAGES 26 AND 27
From the stags of Bull Point, the furthest western point on Rathlin Island, you can enjoy a sea-bird view of the Antrim coast.

RIGHT *Easily recognisable by the shape of its orange beak and colourful webbed feet, the puffin is a friendly-looking seabird.*

BELOW *The stags of Bull Point are nurseries for myriads of seabirds that inhabit them during the nesting season.*

A variety of seabirds nest on the cliffs above the puffins' burrows.

PAGES 32 AND 33 *Seabirds glide above a majestic ocean in search of food for their hungry youngsters.*

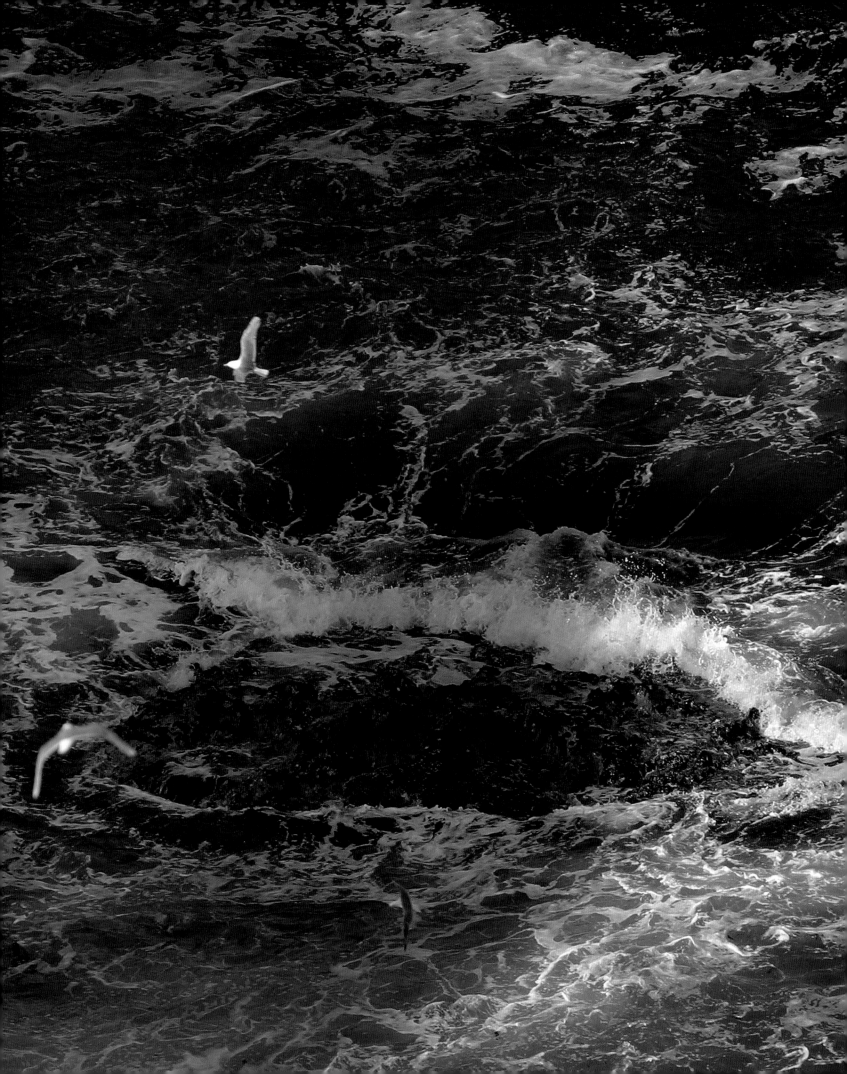

LEFT *Warned of my approach at daybreak by the noise of ferns rubbing against the legs of my trousers, a hen pheasant takes flight in a flurry of startled feathers....*

OPPOSITE TOP AND LEFT *Looking at the ballet of seabirds in front of the cliffs, I feel the size of a grain of sand.*

BELOW *Puffins, like many other seabirds, nest underground. The toes of their webbed feet have sharp claws that are used to scratch out burrows 1 metre (3 to 4 feet) deep where the females lay a single egg. Their favourite nursing grounds are at the very bottom of Bull Point cliffs.*

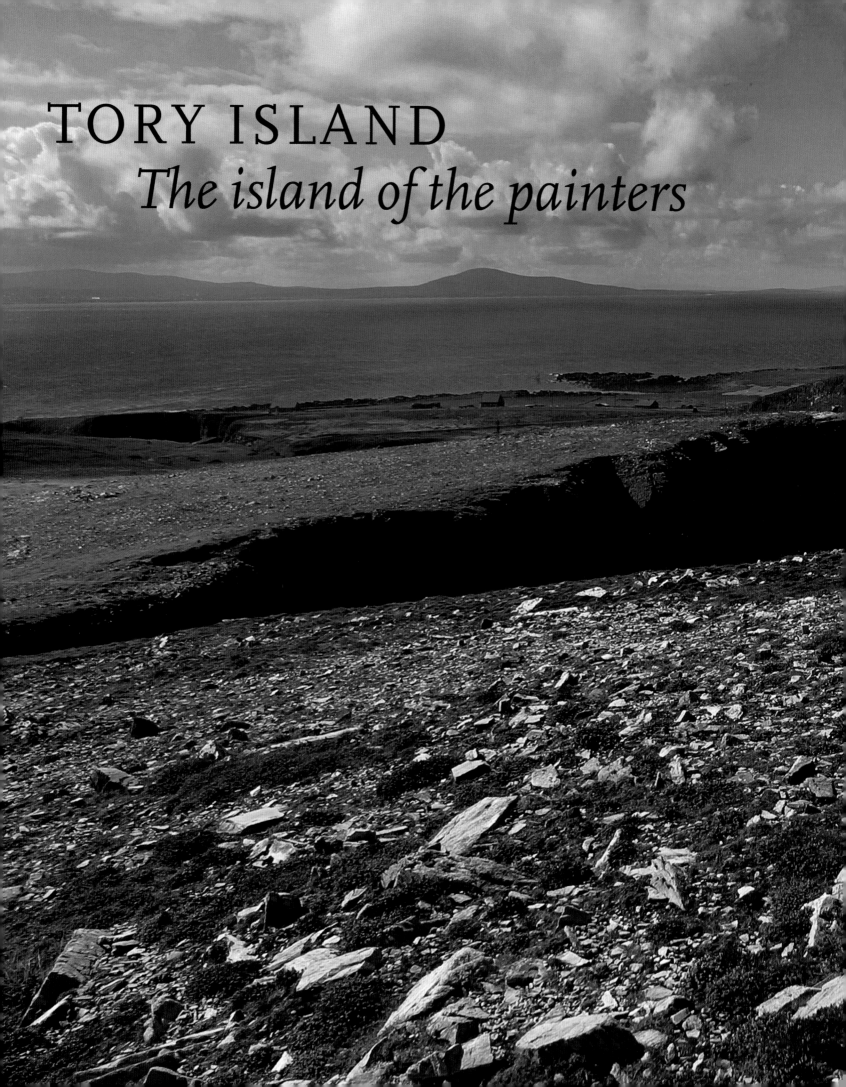

TORY ISLAND
The island of the painters

Tory Island is situated 15 kilometres (9 miles) from the north coast of Donegal and 5 kilometres (3 miles) northwest of Horn Head. The island itself is 5 kilometres long and 1 kilometre (½ a mile) wide and is divided into four 'towns', imaginatively entitled East Town, West Town, Middle Town and New Town.

It can claim four reasons for being famous:

1. It has its very own king.
2. It has a well-known school of primitive painters.
3. It has a tau cross, a stone T-shaped cross dating from the sixth century that could link the Coptic Church to Ireland.
4. It has its own cure for rats.

The king, Patsy Dan Rodgers, is a wee man with a cap who welcomes all newcomers to the harbour. If you are a man, you'll be given a firm handshake and, if you're a woman, you'll have a royal kiss.

In the 1960s, a well-known English painter, Derek Hill, came to live on Tory to paint its extraordinary landscape. In 1968 James Dixon, a local man, who had been watching Hill paint, approached the artist and told him that he, himself, could do better. Hill challenged him to do so, and gave him paints and brushes. Dixon

One of the first primitive paintings of Tory, signed James Rodgers 'The Yank'. There were so many James Rodgers that each of them had a nickname.

> In the 1960s, a well-known English painter, Derek Hill, came to live on Tory to paint its extraordinary landscape.... He inspired other islanders...[and] left behind a thriving 'primitive' painting school.

refused the brushes, saying he would make his own from the hairs of his donkey's tail. He did and Derek was very impressed with the resulting paintings. He inspired other islanders, including Patsy Dan Rodgers, the king. Sadly, Hill passed away, but left behind him a thriving 'primitive' painting school.

The tau cross is the only one found in Ireland. That shape is well known in Egypt and some old sculptures found depicting St Anthony and Paul of Thebus sharing bread in the desert gave some people the idea that the Coptic religion and Ireland were connected somehow.

St Columbkille features prominently in the Christian legends of the sixth century. It is said that, from the top of Muckish on the

Donegal mainland, he looked for a place where he could build a church. He decided to throw a javelin and to build it where it landed. The spot where it fell, on Tory, is still pointed out today. Dugan, a man with dark features, was the first person to help the saint in his project. As a reward, the saint gave him and his descendants the power of banishing the rats.

The Dugan family is still represented on the island today. A handful of clay, collected only by the family in the ruins of the old church, will be given to whoever asks for it with the following words: 'In the name of God, give me some Tory clay.' It is said that, wherever you scatter that clay, rats will disappear for ever.

In the 1970s, as the old staples of fishing and farming slowly died out, survival on the island became increasingly difficult. The community's long presence on Tory nearly came to an end altogether in 1974, when a massive storm convinced some islanders, and some Dublin politicians, that the time had come to abandon ship. During that winter, a seemingly eternal storm swept in off the north Atlantic and battered the island for more than eight weeks, severing every form of communication, even helicopters.

The helpless isolation was more than some islanders could bear. Ten families moved to the Donegal mainland, and others seriously considered doing the same. It was without doubt the island's darkest hour, and a Blasket-style evacuation seemed a real possibility. Some islanders, though, were determined to stay and managed to persuade the Government to help them design a new life for themselves on the island. Thanks to massive investment, a brand new harbour, protective wall and a hotel have been built in recent years. Tourism has played a vital part in the island's survival and the population has now stabilized. The very successful painters – such as the most famous, James Dixon, Patsy Dan Rodgers, Anton Mehan and Rory Rodgers – have their works exhibited all over the world.

The cliffs of Tórmore have given their name to the new island ferry that links Tory to Magheroarrty pier.

Protected from wind and showery weather, Anton Mehan, one of the Tory painters, paints his beloved cliffs from the cab of his tractor.

PAGES 36 AND 37 Anton Mehan surveys the scene near the wishing stone on the East Town, his favourite subject for painting.

A brand new pier and protective wall have just been erected in the West Town of Tory.

Painter Patsy Dan Rodgers, the king of Tory.

*A roadside shrine
to the Virgin Mary.*

Painter Anton Mehan in front of Tory's art gallery.

Tory's islanders have adopted their very own pace of life.

LEFT *Autumnal sunset. When the sky is red on the horizon, it is said that the patron saint of children, St Nicholas, is baking cakes in preparation for 9 December, the feast that bears his name.*

BELOW *One of the many small islands whose name I forgot.*

ABOVE *West Town, seen from Tórmore.*

LEFT *For many years, this old torpedo was the favourite toy of the island's children. It is now used to mark the divide between East Town and West Town.*

ABOVE *The only road on Tory brings you right into the clouds.*

RIGHT *It was in the bogs near Bloody Foreland that I found these brothers at work.*

ABOVE *There is no more turf to be cut on Tory and it is now the mainland that has to provide some of the fuel for the islanders.*

LEFT *Sunshine lights up rusty car wrecks in the bogs of Bloody Foreland.*

OWEY ISLAND
Island of the sheep

Today, my friend Mick McGinley invites me to Owey Island. We met in the 1960s in Killybegs.

Mick, a fishing skipper, spent all his life at sea. He recently lost a man from his boat in a stupid accident and cannot get over it. He has packed in fishing, sold the boat and is now working as a remedial teacher in a local primary school.

Owey, a small island in northwest Donegal, is only one kilometre (half a mile) from shore. Every year when the weather is good enough, islanders get together to shear the sheep that they keep on the island in order to keep a claim to the land. The island was left vacant in 1977 and has a unique status. In 1927 a local judge decided that its inhabitants did not have to pay taxes and declared Owey an independent republic.

Although they now all live on the mainland, some islanders have done up their houses on the island. Others, like Mick, go and spend quality time there, in the summer and at weekends.

Josie Boyle, the local lobsterman ferries us across in his punt. He knows the lobster holes like the back of his hand. His great-grandfather, grandfather and father have passed all their knowledge on to him. Travelling to Owey is like time travel. Lying close to a modern eighteen-hole golf course, the island is strangely quiet and wild, yet, you have the feeling that life in it could be reborn at any moment. The school dominates the island from its roofless grey walls. If you close your eyes for a while, you'll imagine children's joyous cries drifting in and out of your ears on the wind....

Anthony has let his dog Rusty round up the sheep. He is a great dog and has them, panting, in no time, right into the entrance gap of a makeshift pen.

The rain is falling incessantly and the men work in silence. The rough, oily wool is shorn from the sheep and they find themselves naked, shivering and bare like squirming maggots.

Our soaked shirts are glued to our skin. A sheep escapes and, like a kangaroo, jumps high over a fence.' 'He must thinks he is in Australia, that one,' quips the voice of the schoolmaster. Everyone laughs.

When the shearing is over, Mick shows me the house where he slept, as a kid, with his grandmother. The bed is still there. He is fixing the cottage at present and has put in new windows and doors. He'll spend a month working on it before returning to his teaching job.

We are all too wet to stay behind and climb down the slippery steps back to the boat. Anthony is taking three ewes with him as pay for his shearing work. To make us all laugh, Greta, Josie's wife, pretends to board a young man's boat. 'It's time I changed,' she says, 'Mine is all used up.'

Boats are leaving, one to the right, one to the left...a lone sheep is bleating from the old schoolhouse steps. They are kings again of the independent republic of Owey Island.

My friend Mick McGinley lands on the island where he was born.

Every year when the weather is good enough, islanders get together to shear the sheep.... The island was left vacant in 1977.... In 1927 a local judge...declared Owey an independent republic.

PAGES 46 AND 47 *Owey Island's small harbour provides great shelter.*

Once a year the communal sheep shearing brings all the islanders together.

Last summer Mick has started
doing up his own place.

Soaked to the skin, men work in silence and the sheep breathe heavily.

Greta.

Josie.

A sheep escapes, and, like a kangaroo, jumps over the fence.

Sheep are not voluntary seafarers...
some are taken ashore as payment
for the shearer.

ARANMORE ISLAND
The island of the immigrants

The island of Aranmore is the largest of a group of little islands off 'the Rosses', a very indented part of Donegal's northwest coast. Five kilometres (3 miles) long and 4 kilometres (2¹⁄₂ miles) wide, it is 4 kilometres from the mainland. The census of 1834 recorded a population of 1,141. At the end of the seventeenth century, the herring fishery employed 1,000 people in this region, with a fleet of 400 sailing boats.

In 1851 the landowner of the time, a certain John Charley of Londonderry, found it necessary to evict 160 persons, while famine destroyed a large part of the population. An Act of British Parliament had recently stipulated that landowners were responsible for their tenants. As the tenants could no longer pay their way, and it would have cost the landowners £5 a year to keep each of them alive in the poorhouse, they found it more economical to pay for the passage of their tenants on a sailing ship, destination America.

Many of the inhabitants of Aranmore gathered on Castor Island in Lake Michigan. In 1866 fifty-two Irish families were to be found there, and to this day the names Boyle, Gallagher and McCauley are to be encountered on both islands. The two islands were twinned in 2000.

Nowadays, the population is struggling to maintain itself. Many come back after a life of labouring abroad (the men of the Rosses are known as 'the Tunnel Tigers', as many Aranmore men worked on the Channel tunnel, among other projects). They retire to a modernized former family home or to a new bungalow. There is not a lot to do:

they raise a few sheep...play a little music, catch the dinner, gather blackberries... and watch a lot of television....

Aranmore could no longer live from fishing. It is so close to the mainland coast of Donegal that it is very easy to reach it. Holiday houses are being built there.

If you want a quiet life, Aranmore is for you. A notice on the shop's door (closed when I knocked) says:

BUSINESS HOURS

WE'RE OPEN
Most days about 9.30 or 10.00,
Occasionally as early as 7.00,
But some days as late as 11.00 or 12.15.

WE'RE CLOSED
About 5.30 or 6.00,
Occasionally about 4.00 or 5.15,
but, sometimes, as late as 11.00 or 12.30.

Some days or afternoons, we aren't here at all
and lately, I have been here just about all the time,
except when I am some place else
but should be here then too.

The teenagers coming home from school at weekends put a bit of life into this island that lives very slowly.

Illanaran Island, on the southwestern point of Aranmore.

PAGES 52 AND 53 *The sky is heavy. Fishing will be good tonight when the tide comes up.*

At the end of the seventeenth century, the herring fishery employed 1,000 people in this region, with a fleet of 400 sailing boats. In 1851... famine destroyed a large part of the population.

Two brothers whom I met on the road invite me into their house. One of them has just returned from Scotland, where he emigrated when he was a kid.
Of all the islands I visited, this one has the friendliest people.

Men butchering their
own sheep.

If you want a quiet life, Aranmore is for you.

A completely restful place for enjoying your retirement.

ABOVE *The notice on the shop's door.*

RIGHT *The tide is up.*

CLARE ISLAND

The island of the wedding

Mary and Darren are getting married today. Mary, a well-known traditional musician, has asked me to take the wedding pictures for the family.

Darren and I are both disciples of the barstool. We always find ourselves drinking together when Mary and her group are playing. They have chosen Clare Island for their big day.

Clare Island and Inishbofin Island, her neighbour, are both well known for the 'craic'. As neither of them has a policeman, the opening hours of bars and hotels are pretty elastic. If the guards want the law to be respected, they have to come from the mainland on the island ferry. As the owner of the bar skippers the island's ferry, there are no surprises.

The day before the wedding, Mary and Darren decorate the church. Mattie, their Labrador bitch, gives them a hand. She eats every flower she can get her teeth into...

The weather is gorgeous and we walk around the island. The view from the top of the cliffs would take your breath away. We sit for a while on a wall of the western lighthouse that is no longer in use. A Belgian couple bought it a decade ago and transformed it into a guest house. They spent a fortune doing it up and were very popular with the islanders. Alas, they recently sold it to an heiress. She seldom visits and is not the most popular person on the island.

After supper, we all retire early to save our energy. A full gale is blowing the next morning and we are panicking as it is not known whether the ferry will be able to travel and bring the guests.... Luckily, by mid morning, it quietens down for long enough to bring everyone safely to the island.

We are all wearing our best clothes and the sombre, overdramatic priest is no match for the overall good mood. Tears are pouring out of everyone's eyes as Pauline Scanlon sings a heart-rending song from the back of the church. My vision is blurred and I cannot see through my camera for a while. The young couple is glowing and they are driven to the hotel in a gennet and cart....

In Ireland, we are known to be able to throw a party at the drop of a hat and we have a well-known saying: 'When are you going to give us a day out?' This is a common way to address those who have been courting for a while. We love weddings, here, especially in the country. It is a way to forget for a while the monotony of day-to-day life and celebrate the joys of life with your neighbours – often to excess....

There is such a good vibe in the air and we are all so happy to be together that some of us decide to stay on the island a while longer – for three extra days and three extra nights – as far as I am concerned.

Clare Island survives because of tourism and its elastic opening hours. Every few months they hold a bachelors' weekend at the hotel and the women outnumber men two to one. Liam, the owner's son, is very good-looking and tells me those weekends are very difficult for him. He stays hidden from Friday night to Monday morning....

PAGES 58 AND 59 *On their big day on Clare Island, Mary and Darren have a lift from the church with the local gennet driver.*

Clare Island and Inishbofin Island, her neighbour, are both well known for the 'craic'. As neither of them has a policeman, the opening hours of bars and hotels are pretty elastic.

Mary and Darren on their wedding day.

The lighthouse, reconverted into a bed and breakfast by a Belgian couple, has been sold to a wealthy woman, who lives elsewhere.

The day before the wedding, Mary and Darren decorate the church with flowers. Mattie, their bitch, helps out by eating every flower in sight....

INISHTURK

Fishermen's island

I nishturk means the island of the hog, although there aren't any to be found there now. I have been meaning to get back there for ages and today I am boarding the ferry from Roonagh pier.

Jack is the skipper–owner of the ferry, the *Atlantic Queen*. There are a dozen of us aboard, two island families coming back from their weekly shopping in Westport and a few visitors. It is a beautiful day and the boat travels so fast that you have the feeling we are sailing above the waves.

On deck, little blobs of yellow foam are trembling and sparkling in the sunshine. The boat is jumping like a greyhound every time we hit a bigger wave. Jack and his crewman, Eamon, cast a vacant look at the sea ahead of us. They have recognized me, as I used to fish in these waters twenty years ago on a boat from Donegal.

We are chitchatting about fishing and people we know. I explain to Jack that I am taking pictures of islands for a book and that I am here to photograph the local fishermen. He tells me that I am in luck – the weather is good and, after his supper, he is going to lift pots with Eamon in his new curragh. 'May I join you?' "Sure, if you haven't lost your sea legs...we have lots of gear to haul.'

Wearing his elegant blue gloves, Jack, the skipper of the ferry, lifts up his lobster pots.

The sun is already low in the sky when we reach the first fleet of pots. Jack motors expertly to the red buoy that signals the end of the gear....

While Jack goes home, I find a bed for the night with Mary and Bill Heanue. Bill is also a fisherman and Mary, the local cooperative's secretary, runs a marvellous bed and breakfast. I don't know how she finds the time with all the kids running around the house.

I put on my oilskins and find Jack and Eamon waiting for me at the pier. Jack has a brand new curragh, *The St Patrick*. It was built on a neighbouring island and is much sturdier than the local boats built out of tarred canvas. This one is made of larch planks and is much heavier.

The sun is already low in the sky when we reach the first fleet of pots. Jack motors expertly to the red buoy that signals the end of the gear and Eamon retrieves it by hand. The head rope is fed in the hauler that lifts the pots, while Eamon coils it carefully in neat rows.

Once aboard, the pots have to be emptied, re-baited and stored perfectly so that enough room is left for the whole fleet of pots. The lobsters are kept under a wet cloth and the undersized ones are thrown back into the sea to grow some more.

After a long day's work, the arms that do the lifting are aching. There are ten fleets of pots to lift and the work is dangerous and difficult. There is not much room in a small curragh that is being tossed about

on the waves. Everyone has to be very careful and keep an eye open for mishaps. Accidents happen very quickly at sea...and most fishermen cannot swim. Most prefer not to learn: they say that, if they don't learn to swim, they would sink quickly if they fell overboard in a heavy sea to a near-certain death. The Government has ordered that life jackets be worn, but they are so cumbersome that they are seldom put on.

The weather being so kind, we fish till late, and other boats motor back to the island pier. I recognize some faces and we greet each other in silence. Everyone is tired. Mary cooks some ray wings that Bill brought back and some crabs that Jack gave me. Delicious.

Inishturk has two harbours. The main one is the centre of all activities on the island. Boats are coming and going every day. The other harbour is a natural gap in the cliffs that opens on to a quiet and shallow lagoon: Portoon. Half a dozen curraghs fish from there. Inishturk is unique – everyone seems to be active and working and it is a very vibrant community of some eighty people. The national primary school boasts two schoolteachers for a handful of happy kids. The older ones go to school on the mainland and return for most weekends. In summer, when everyone is home, the population grows by thirty per cent.

The next day, I join an old fishing colleague Mick O'Toole and his son Anthony to go and lift some bait nets. The sea is calm and, while Anthony works on deck, Mick and I chat in the wheelhouse. It feels good to be alive, here. The island has four bed and breakfasts, a post office, a social club, the local pub and communal hall, a chapel and a graveyard.

The courageous will to work in all its inhabitants makes Inishturk the most prosperous island I have visited. I mean spiritual prosperity as well as material.

Today is market day in Roonagh. Warmed by an early summer sun, fishermen are preparing their catches for market.

ABOVE *Eamon's fingers are caught by a baby crab.*

LEFT *Eamon shoots the pots while Jack directs the operation from the outboard's tiller.*

PAGES 62 AND 63 *Emerging out of the morning mist, the top of Sheeffrey Mountain overlooks the little island of Inishturk.*

Father and son steer their curragh out of Portoon, Inishturk's natural harbour.

Fishermen's bothies.

Inishturk's harbour.

LEFT *Bill Heanue's boat steaming alongside Ballybeg Island.*

PAGES 68 AND 69 *Shimmering colours on the rocks at the bottom of Inishturk's cliff.*

LEFT *A lobster claw in a fisherman's keep.*

BELOW *Crayfish.*

OPPOSITE *Dog fish, black pollocks, yellow pollocks, lings, wrasse – everything is used to bait the local aristocrats: crayfish and lobsters.*

ABOVE *Bernard Heanue is delighted with these two big lobsters, caught in a hole whose location is kept top secret.*

LEFT *At the market in Roonagh, a fisherman keeps a close eye on the pocket calculator of a buyer from Brittany.*

LEFT *The curraghs are made of tarred cloth, stretched on a light wooden frame. They are very light and do not plough into the waves but ride upon them.*

BELOW *Noel unloads crayfish and lobster boxes on Roonagh pier.*

FRIAR ISLAND
The island of the big seal

With the tanks full and the food cupboard replenished, we set sail for Friar Island, an inhabited island. Unlike its depressing neighbour, Inishshark, Friar is beautiful and wild. It is an odd shape and seems to be divided into four parts. The water is crystal clear and everything here seems healthy. The monk or hermit who lived here must have given extra good vibrations to the animals and plants that inhabit it (or vice versa).

A large seal swims quietly between the rocks, watching my every move. It goes back and forth for more than one hour. From time to time it dives after a fish, only to emerge a minute later, blowing air noisily. It looks at me quietly before resuming its swimming. The birds also seem to be unafraid and land close to me to have a good look and sing me a little song.

Seaweed waves silently in the swell and thousands of tiny fish are playing hide and seek, creating a shower of little shiny silver ringlets when they touch the surface.

The island has a beautiful smell, the sounds are harmonious and the colours delicate. It is a paradise for my senses. After long hours spent at sea, where everything moves constantly and the water, the sky and the boat become your universe, Friar Island is heaven for an afternoon. I wanted to camp there overnight but Joe tells me the forecast is not good and we had better hurry and go and shelter off Inishturk if we want to get there in time for Caher Island's pilgrimage.

I am sorry to leave my animal companions and the island. A few dolphins join us for a while before diving in front of our bow to follow a little fishing boat going in the other direction....

Refreshed, Joe comes back from his morning dive.

A few dolphins join us for a while before diving in front of our bow to join a little fishing boat going in the other direction...

PAGES 74 AND 75 *Early morning in the mist of Inishbofin. Suddenly Joe plunges into the water. It happens so quickly that I have no time to react. I push on the shutter button a fraction of a second too late and take a very good picture of the spray shooting up in the air in front of a misty castle...with no evidence of Joe.*

While going about its business in Friar Island, a large seal swims peacefully among the rocks but never once lets its eyes off me.

Lichen and moss grow happily on Friar Island.

PAGES 78 AND 79 *The water is crystal clear and the place feels really healthy.*

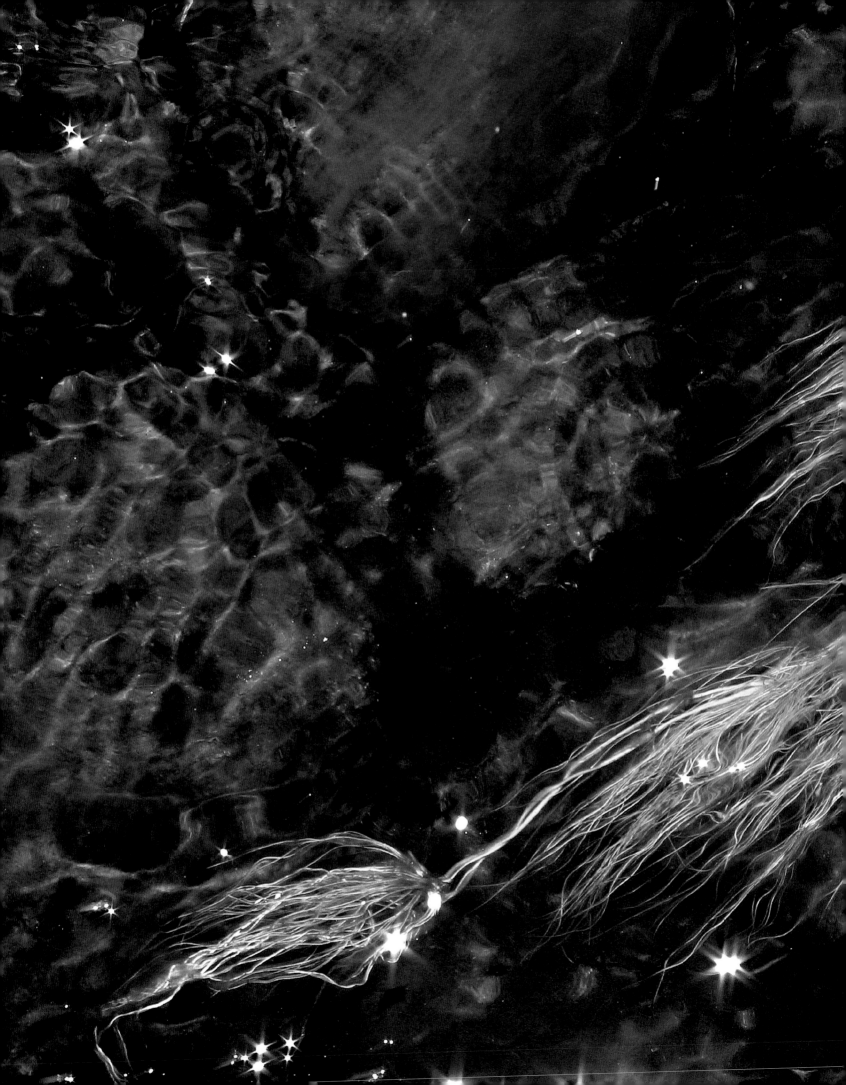

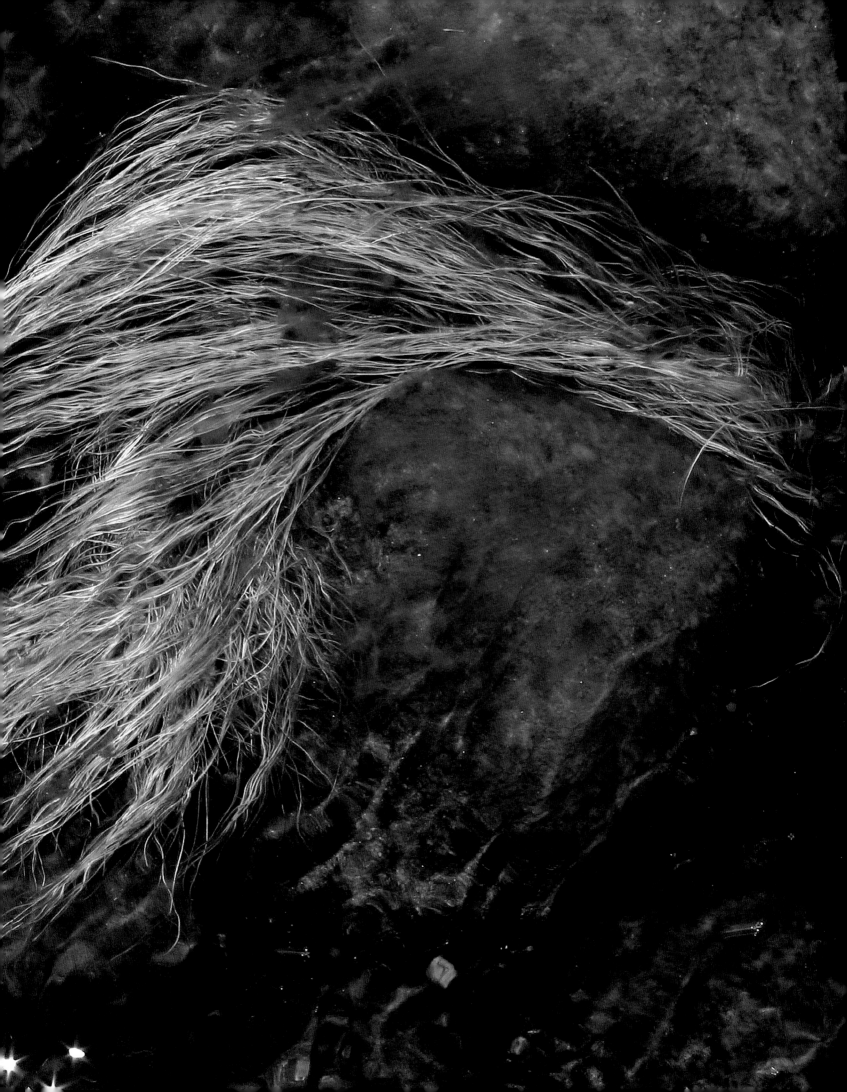

*Underneath sparkling, starry waters,
seaweed slowly undulates. Crowning every
rock, numerous pieces of moss and lichen
bear witness to the purity of the air.*

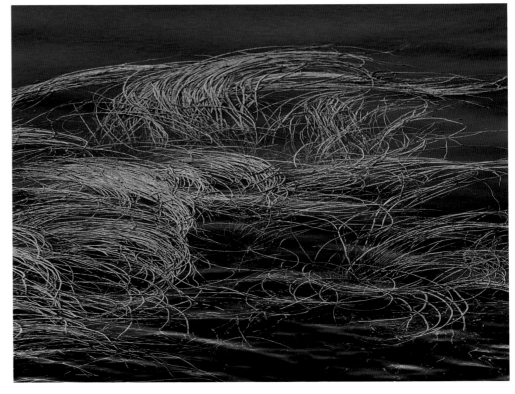

Because of its strange shape, Friar Island looks as though it is split into four different sections.

INISHSHARK
The abandoned island

When he cast a last long look on his island before leaving it for ever, in 1960, Thomas Lacey declared, with a tear glistening at the corner of the eye: 'It only gave us poverty and hard labour and took two of my sons.' His two sons had drowned eleven years before on their way back to the island.

In 1958 a Shark man had died of appendicitis because it took five days before word of his plight could be sent to the mainland. Thomas Lacey continued: 'Last winter, in November and December, we were without tea, sugar, tobacco and paraffin for six weeks. The wind was howling and the waves crashed on the roof.' It was the drop that overfilled the bucket. The islanders asked the Government to take them off the island and rehouse them on the mainland. Lacey commented: 'I have wanted to leave for years. The tear you see on my cheek is a tear of the past, for the loss of my sons. It isn't today's tear.'

We sat on a wardrobe and watched the twelve inhabitable but untenable houses of Shark fade out of life.

Nature slowly reconquers an island that was vacated in the 1960s.

Today, 27 October 1960, twenty-three survivors, members of six families are leaving the island for ever. This is how Dixon Scott described the exodus in the *Daily Mirror*:

The sun shone beautifully. The breeze came softly from the east and the Atlantic only rippled instead of roaring. It was a perfect day for the death of an island.

So, on this rare, fine morning, four fishing smacks left the neighbouring island of Bofin on the last mercy mission to Shark. The fleet – St John, St Winifred, Topaz and Lilly – was commanded by young Father Flannery, the island's priest, acting as agent for the Government. Off came Father Flannery's dog collar and jacket as we stepped on to Shark's landing stage. 'Right, lads, let's get moving!' he said. Soon men, women and children were staggering along the stony 500 yards between their cottages and the landing stage with their burdens, back-breaking, bizarre, and one, at least, bonny.... A huge, homemade wardrobe lashed to the shoulders of fifty-three-years-old Michael Cloonan. A dark brown cat in an old blackened cooking pot, with the lid half tied down.... Eleven-months-old baby Anne Lacey in the arms of her mother... Anne Murray's geraniums, hens in baskets, geese in sacks, straw brooms and string-tied suitcases, iron bed-steads and baths.... Thirteen cows, twelve dogs, ten donkeys. Eight more cats, scores of hens, a hundred sheep, a stack of hay – and a tear in the eye of Thomas Lacey, the elder. They all came down to the water's edge of Shark for the last time. Ten-years-old Philomena Murray lingered to the last in the schoolroom she shared with four other island children before teacher Rose McGarry went sick to the mainland a month ago. But her search on the big map of Ireland over the fireplace was for the spot in Connemara where her new home would be.... 'This is a happy day for us,' she said simply. I sailed in the Noah's Ark armada with old Thomas Lacey's third son, Thomas Joseph, and his wife and baby. 'Why should I not be happy to be going?' said Thomas, 73, grandfather of baby Anne Lacey and 'father' of the island. I have wanted to leave for years. We sat on a wardrobe and watched the twelve inhabitable but untenable houses of Shark fade out of life. 'That island is finished,' said Thomas Joseph, turning his back on it and pulling noisily on his pipe. His baby whimpered. At Cleggan, on the mainland, I watched him accept the key to the new life that the Irish Government has provided for each of the six Shark families. There was a brand new bungalow by the sea, eight acres of land, a share in the grazing rights on a mountain and a shave of a bog for digging peat. It was cheaper for the Government to do this than to sink many thousands of pounds into a new harbour for Shark. Thomas Joseph looked so please[d] it seemed that the sea, even in victory, had somehow been cheated. BUT SHARK IS, OF COURSE, DEAD.

Today Shark is deserted. I spent a day there and I became physically moved and emotional when I entered the ruins of houses that cried of poverty and were inhabited by the carcasses of dead sheep.

It was with great relief that I rowed back to the *Anna M*, ready to set sail to happier lands.

On leaving the island, Thomas Lacey, aged 73, declared: 'I am glad to turn my back on it for ever!'

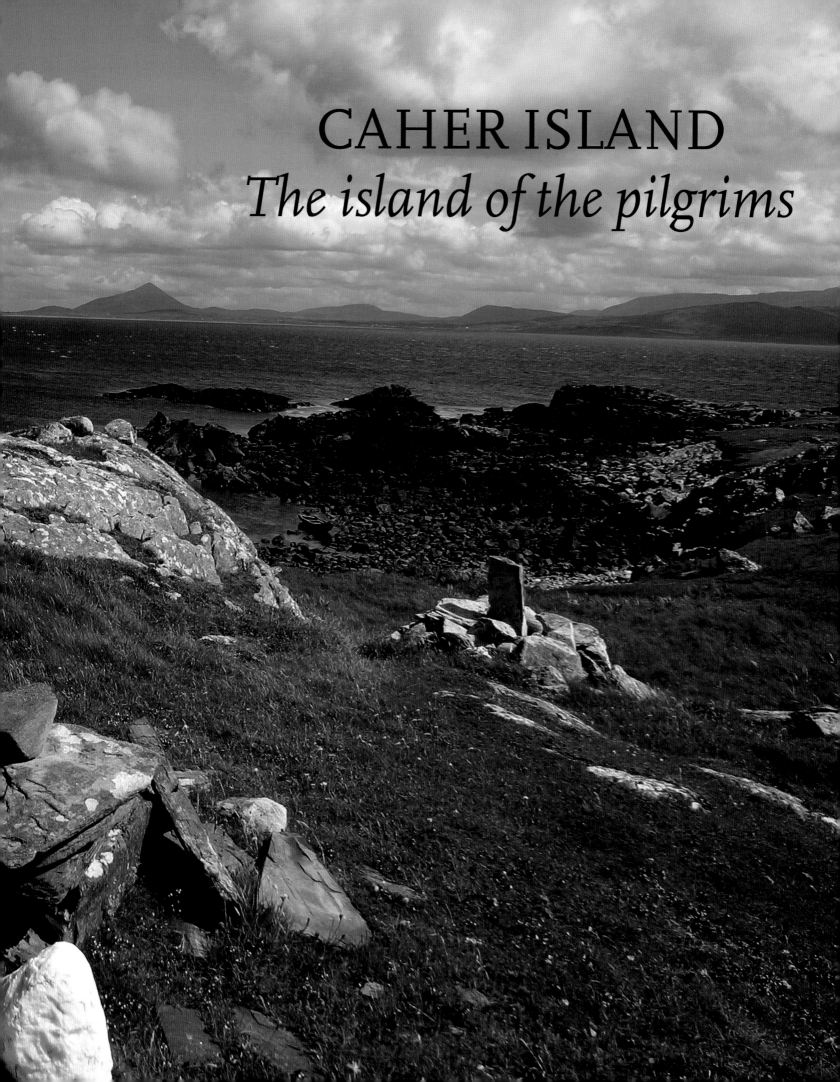

CAHER ISLAND
The island of the pilgrims

It is on the most inaccessible islands, ceaselessly attacked by the fury of the winds and waves of the Atlantic, that there are still the ruins of churches, monasteries and hermitages from early Christian times.

The one I cherish most is Caher Island. It is called 'the ring-fort of the saints'. There are the ruins of a little church, ancient tombstones and stone crosses. Owing to the shapes of the stones and to their worn, barely discernible carvings, especially the Dolphin Stone, archaeologists and historians have been able to establish direct links between some holy places on the continent and this little island at the mouth of Clew Bay, as well as between the early illuminated manuscripts and metal crosses and the sculptured stones of Caher. Situated directly beneath the great peak of Croagh Patrick, Caher Island is the destination for a pilgrimage made on 15 August, feast of the Assumption of Our Lady, if the sea permits.

It is said that St Patrick spent the forty days and forty nights before Easter on the summit of the mountain bearing his name. In that place he confronted all his inner demons, and came down radiant and bursting with energy. The year was 441. In the next twenty years, he founded many monasteries, divided the country into dioceses and built up the Church there.

Today is 15 August 2004, and I am awoken by sunshine. The sea is flat calm. Our sailing boat is anchored off Inishturk, and Bernard, on his way out to lift his lobster pots in a blue curragh, brings us fresh bread that, Phil, his wife has baked for us. We take our breakfast on the deck. The island is still asleep. It is six in the morning.

Pilgrims arrive on the island on 15 August.

PAGES 86 AND 87 Caher Island is called 'Cathair na Naomh' (the Saint's Cove). The hermitage of Caher dates to the earliest centuries of Christianity. Among the ruins of the church, stone slabs and cross slabs engraved with Celtic ornaments, particularly the Dolphin Stone that dates from the sixth or seventh century. The pointed hill on the horizon is the famous Croagh Patrick.

> It is on the most inaccessible islands, ceaselessly attacked by the fury of the winds and waves of the Atlantic, that there are still the ruins of churches, monasteries and hermitages from early Christian times.

At eleven o'clock, we are already anchored at Caher. Lying on deck and rocked by a slight swell, we observe the far-off comings and goings of fishing boats as they ply between the islands gathering pilgrims.

All of a sudden the seals, which had been basking in the sun while keeping an eye on us from the corner of their moustaches, disappear…. A minute later the *Atlantic Queen* appears behind the rocks. She is scattering spray, making fifteen knots. Soon the passengers climb aboard the *St Patrick*, which Jack skilfully steers between the reefs so as to leave them on the island. A rainbow of colour appears there; all the boats arrive and two hundred people are clinging to the steep rocks as they climb to the little church. The young priest, Father Michael Mannion, welcomes us, thanks everyone for coming and invites us to recollect ourselves in silence, before celebrating the most authentic Mass that I ever attended.

Touched by this authenticity, by the past and the sacredness of the place, we have the impression of being united in the silence. Only a skylark, high above our heads, salutes us with its shrill calls. After the communion, a professor of archaeology gives us a little talk on the history of Caher.

Then everyone gets back on board the boat that had brought them. The tide has risen so that the largest of them, the Clare Island ferry, can go so close to the island that she can jam herself between the rocks. You have to do the splits to step across the 2 metres (6½ feet) that separate her from the land. A pair of trousers rips and everyone bursts out laughing noisily.

They all go away. The seals, reassured, haul themselves back on to their favourite rocks. Joe and I, back on the deck of our boat, stay another hour to savour what this marvellous place has to offer.

The morning of 15 August pilgrims arrive on ferries and fishing boats before being brought ashore on curraghs.

RIGHT *Warmed by the sun, pilgrims enjoy the stunning landscape, before returning to the boats that brought them there.*

BELOW *An archaeologist explains the significance of the Dolphin Stone for us.*

Young Father Mannion celebrates Mass. The trills of the skylark, high above our heads, are the only sounds to break the sacred silence that unites us all for an instant.

Those with short legs have to do the splits to board their floating taxis.

It is rumoured that St Patrick was buried under this simple carved slab.

MAYFLIES ISLANDS
The islands of the mayflies

L ough Arrow, Lough Carragh, Lough Conn, Lough Corrib and Lough Mask – so many names that fill the dreams of entomologists, poets and trout fishermen. 'The fly is up!' This short sentence is going to create chaos among the craziest of us in the lake lands of Ireland.

One, and then another, and then millions, of nymphs leave the womb of the lake's depth and undulate towards the surface, where they begin their hatching process. First the legs, then the body and, eventually, in a final effort, the wings appear out of their now empty birthing envelope, 'the shuck'. Infused with new life, the trembling bodies are capped with wings of yellow green that resemble striped semi-translucent half parachutes. Helped by wind and waves, they dry themselves for a moment before taking off to the shelter of the bushes on the lakeshore.

If it is windy and the water surface is choppy, their first flight will be easy. If it is completely calm and the lake is like a mirror, they will find it difficult to break the surface tension and will be easy prey for trout, seagulls, merganser ducks and even swans....

Tommy Flynn, a wee capped man who lives on the shores of Lough Arrow in Co. Sligo, knows that when his lilac bush is in flower, the fly will hatch within forty-eight hours. Wherever you are and whoever

One more fly in the dapping box.

Tommy Flynn...knows that when his lilac bush is in flower, the fly will hatch within forty-eight hours...

you are, you will receive the telegram you have been waiting for if you left your address and a few pounds to Tommy the year before: 'The fly is up, Tommy.' Gynaecologist in New York, garage owner in Dublin, or poet in London, everybody will leave wives, children and work commitments behind.

Caravans, trailers, boats, engines and lakeside bed and breakfast will spring suddenly to life. The fly does not wait. If an east or northerly wind comes and cool everything down, it will all end before it really had time to begin. The ideal weather for the hatch is a moderate southwesterly wind that warms up the air and brings light grey clouds bursting with rain.

Once the green fly has taken shelter on the bushes, nature performs a second miracle: the fly turns dark grey, flattens her wings on her abdomen and transforms herself a second time. A beautiful slim fly with a pearl body and translucent fragile wings emerges out of a juicy green adolescence that lasted all of twenty-four hours. Equipped with brand new wings, millions of 'black gnats', as we call them, start their wedding dance, sheltered from wind and rain.

They fly up a few metres before gracefully falling back the same

few metres over and over again, alongside hazel and may bushes. Nature has given them just one day to transform themselves into their adult bodies, dance, copulate and lay the eggs that will ensure their line continues.

Drunk with dance and spring weather, the females fly at dusk towards the water and mate in the air, with thousands of little males, who, like kamikaze flying sperm, drop dead once their deed is accomplished. The females fall graciously, and, shivering, dip their little abdomens in the water. They deposit thousands of eggs that slowly drift down to the mud at the bottom. There they will slowly transform themselves and spring back to life again in a year or two. The mayfly is a miracle of life. Beautiful and delicate, it has no apparent purpose. Trout, seagulls and fishermen could very well live without it.

Yet nature is generous and does not follow reason. Every year, between 15 May and 15 June, I throw my 'shuck' and responsibilities to the wind and join my friend Paul on Lyckle's Island in Lough Arrow.

I will borrow a few words from an enlightened poet friend of mine, Michael Murphy, who no longer fishes:

Hatching mayflies are fluttering on the sweet breath of spring. Scattered by the spendthrift hand of nature, small miracles of life, they come to rest upon the boat. Rocking on a gentle swell, enveloped in the sudden quiet of a silenced outboard engine, you look around you at encircling hills that are mottled with cloud shadows. You are looking on the lake again, oars dipping to scatter reflections and the fly is up. Life is reborn through spring and beneath the mayfly that are trembling into flight on the surface film move the trout. Bronzed, speckled with gold and red, trout that rise to snatch your fly....

At last, it's out on the water with a gentle breeze that is just right for dapping. This is what you might call living, angst and alienation how are you. Above your head, the clouds filling out like God's washing, high and immaculate and all around the water shimmers with reflections.

Then the dapping rod bends, the reel spins and the first trout is on...

With dapping boxes under the arm, Martin O'Sullivan and Jimmy Walsh, lifetime fishing partners, pick up fresh flies on the bushes. Dapping the natural insect is the typical Irish method used to catch the speckled trout that feed on them to a frenzy.

Once hatched out of the water, the green mayfly seeks shelter on the bushes where it will transform itself into a black fly. It is the juicy green mayfly that is used for dapping.

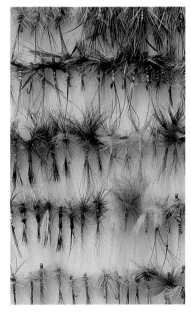

Some of the artificial mayflies tied by my friend John Weir.

PAGES 92 AND 93 Lough Corrib in Co. Galway counts 365 islands, one for every day of the year.

Paul and Emmet wait for a fall of spents...once mated, female black flies lay their eggs on the surface.
While doing so, they struggle and hop and it is their dying motions that attract the bigger fishes.

From his cottage's door on Lyckle's Island, in Lough
Arrow, Co. Sligo, my friend Paul watches the sky
for rain to find out whether flies are going to hatch.

This freshly hatched green fly cannot take off, as there is no wind.
It is caught in the surface tension.

ABOVE *Paul with a fine wild Lough Arrow trout.*

RIGHT *'The bog bank', one of my favourite spots on a secret lake.*

PAGES 98 AND 99 *A great spot for a house on a small island in Lough Corrib. The gorse is in flower, the fly is up.*

ABOVE *Two ancient oak trees and seven sleepy sheep at dawn on Variant's Island, Lough Arrow.*

LEFT *Stones, branches and water. From these three elements, nature creates a unique masterpiece that I have the cheek to capture (Lyckle's Island, Lough Arrow).*

RIGHT *A millionaire's mansion on one of the many islands of Lough Corrib.*

BELOW *Heaven on earth: Lough Corrib in May.*

Reeds, at the bog banks, caress the sides of my boat.

Wearing shoes made of green moss, the centenarian roots of an oak tree on Lyckle's Island make me feel humble.

ABOVE AND BELOW *Drunk with fresh sap, thousands of May bushes laden with white flowers are singing, 'It is springtime' on the islands of Lough Corrib.*

Every morning, in front of Paul's house, a cheeky chaffinch comes and asks for its breakfast.

ABOVE *Paul casting at dusk.*

RIGHT *With dinner on his shoulder, Paul walks back to his house on the island.*

LEFT AND BELOW *We smoke the trouts we catch.*

BELOW *I believe you have never tasted anything as delicious. After a long day in the fresh air, a wild Lough Arrow trout smoked with oak shavings, a cool bottle of white wine, candlelight and a fire in the grate.... Paradise!*

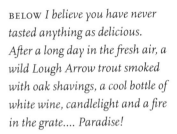

INISHMAAN
The island of the game

The Aran Islands are to be found in the middle of Galway Bay, 30 kilometres (18½ miles) to the north of Co. Clare and 30 kilometres to the south of Connemara. The largest one, Inishmore (Irish Inis Mór, meaning 'the big island'), lies to the north and is very popular with tourists from all over the world who flock to it all year long. Inishmaan (Irish Inis Meáin, meaning 'the middle island') is the quietest and most traditional, and is also my favourite. Inisheer (Irish Inis Oirr, meaning 'the eastern island'), the smallest, is the furthest south and the nearest to the Clare coast. They are all, in fact, part of the Burren and made of limestone. This material consists of thousands of years of hardened marine sediments from the bottom of the ocean that covered them millions of years ago.

Today, 16 March 2003, I am in Rossaveel, taking the ferry for Inishmaan. Its inhabitants are fiercely protective of their island. It is no wonder when you know that every grain of earth to be found there is the product of the toil of countless generations. The seaweed gathered on the shores was brought by those with bare feet or on a donkey's back, if you were lucky to own one, and in heavy baskets to be spread on fields of flat rocks, where, decade after decade, it rotted

Wide as a golf ball, the Cead is a little hazel stick, 15 centimetres (5 ⅞ inches) long, that you hit with a rough bat.

Today is Cead day. The Cead is an ancient game that is only played on Inishmaan, and only on Paddy's Day.

to form this fertile earth. There are only two passengers on the boat bound for Inishmaan: an American, whose wife's parents came from the island, and myself. The ferry comes alongside the island in a heavy swell and it takes the heavy shaking of two men to wake up the prodigal son who had had a bit too much to drink the night before while celebrating his return from America. We carry him like a bag of potatoes and lay him to rest in the shelter of the pier wall among the other cargoes that came on the boat. This boat makes straight for Inisheer and I am left to walk a few steep miles to the house of Máire Pháidín, a beautiful woman in her eighties, who runs a small bed and breakfast next to the church.

Before I have time to unpack my bag, I find myself transformed into a plumber. Máire's range cooker is giving her trouble. Covered in soot, I try, as best as I can, to fix the problem with anything I have to hand. Anything you have to hand is often the only recipe here. Necessity brings out creativity in you when the nearest shop is thirty kilometres away on the other side of a capricious sea that separates you from the mainland. As I have been of some help, Máire fetches some fresh eggs from the henhouse for my supper, while I wash myself.

The next day is a beautiful sunny day. Today is 17 March, the feast day of St Patrick, the patron saint of Ireland, and it is a holiday. Everyone

goes to church to celebrate. Women go in first and most men stay back, as close as they can, to the door. They kneel on their caps, heads bowed. The Mass is in Irish, as this is the native language of the Aran Islands.

When the Mass is over, most people head for the sports ground near the pier. Today is Cead day. The Cead is an ancient game that is only played on Inishmaan, and only on Paddy's Day. The game is very simple. You lay a little piece of carved round stick, the Cead, alongside a flat stone. Armed with another stick, of unknown proportion and thickness, you have to hit the Cead with a gentle, well-calculated tap, to propel it, at arm's length, in front of you. There, suspended in mid air for a second, (see Newton and the apple), you have to hit it with all your strength to send it flying 32 metres (35 yards) further, across an old fishing rope lying on the ground.

I assure you, it is not as simple as it looks. There is a knockout process with several teams of six being eventually whittled down to the last two competing in the final. The game goes on all afternoon. With the Atlantic swell in your back, your head warmed by the spring sunshine, it is a lovely and healthy way to spend St Patrick's Day.

It is the same team, led by Pádraic O Meacháir, that wins for the third time in a row. My American companion from the ferry is in the team and is thrilled to be there. He cannot stop admiring the trophy.

Now that the game is finished, we all head for the pub where the owner fills the cup with a lethal mix of brandy and Guinness. In fact, I think that this is the third, unofficial part of the Cead. All night long, the cup, always half full, makes the rounds. Here too, it is a knockout contest

When I finally get away in the small hours of the morning, I am not the only one having difficulties finding my steps. Somewhere in the dark, ahead of me, I hear two lads who have fallen in the ditch, asking me, in roars of laughter, if I have taken any nice pictures? The next day, at breakfast, I ask Máire why the Cead is only played on St Patrick's Day? 'Sure, isn't as good a day for it as any?' is her short answer....

First, you have to give the Cead a little tap to lift it up in the air…. You then have to hit it with all your strength.

PAGES 106 AND 107 *With the Atlantic surf behind them and the spring sunshine above them, Inishmaan islanders celebrate St Patrick's Day by playing the Cead.*

The winning team for the third year in a row.

ABOVE *In full swing!*

RIGHT AND FAR RIGHT *Liam the Blacám, a friend's son, hitting the Cead in his garden.*

ABOVE *Dara Beag O Fátharta, Breda and Naomi wearing traditional Aran clothes.*

LEFT *A turf fire has a lovely smell and creates an intimate atmosphere.*

PAGES 112 AND 113 *A small derelict thatched cottage: the wild Atlantic winds can reduce the hard labour of generations to nothing in a couple of seasons.*

ABOVE *Máire Pháidín feeding the hens.
I stay with Máire Pháidín when I go to
Inishmaan. I had lost a lens cap the last
time I was there and she returned it to me
with the following note, translated from Irish:
'I found this out in front of the chicken place,
on the windy day, Saturday. It must have
blown from somewhere. I was there often,
and until at midday to feed them, it was
there in front of me. Here it is. Slán, Máire.'*

RIGHT *There is no rush: with a heavy hay bag
on his shoulder, an islander is going to feed his
only cow.*

ABOVE *The stonewalls of Inishmaan are like priceless sculptures. In the background you can see Connor's fort, the largest ring-fort on the island. Little is known about it. Early inhabitants probably built it to protect themselves from pirates and invaders.*

LEFT *This fertile soil results from the hard work of many generations of islanders, who continued to put seaweed on the rocks. After many years the seaweed rotted to produce this rich soil. Each small field is protected like a diamond by countless impeccably kept stonewalls.*

GREAT BLASKET ISLAND
The island of the writers

The Blasket Islands are situated to the west of the famous Dingle peninsula in Co. Kerry. They are just opposite the hamlet of Dunquin, near Slea Head. In front of you, the Great Blasket, with its little whitewashed cottages. To the south, Inish na Bro and Inishvickillane, where a former Irish Taoiseach, Charles Haughey, has a house; to the west, Tearaght, surmounted by its lighthouse, and little Beginish with its sweet grass; to the north, wild Tuaisceart, alias the Bishop, because its profile resembles a recumbent prelate with mitred head. It is a majestic place that you will never forget, if one day, as I hope, your feet happen to take you there....

The Blaskets are famous for their beauty but even more so for their writers. Three of them wrote autobiographies that became literary classics: Tomás O'Crohan (Tomás O'Criomhthain), *The Islandman* (1934); Peig Sayers, *An Old Woman's Reflections* (1978); and Maurice O'Sullivan (Muiris O'Súileabháin), *Twenty Years A'Growing* (1933).

These works, jewels of an oral tradition of storytelling and poetry, transport you like a time-machine into the world in which the writers led their lives. That world was their north, their south, their east and their west. Stuffed full of colourful and humorous expressions, they tell of life within a totally homogenous community, where the people wielded humour like a rapier in the swordplay of their speech. Always preoccupied by the weather of the day, these islanders use the least statement on the matter as an occasion for a verbal joust. Simple in form, these writings are unique, coming from an area of a few square kilometres that contains their whole world.

My friend Joe is an old salt and we have shared lots of sea adventures between us. He just brought the Anna M *back from Venezuela before starting on this little trip with me. The sea clears up the eyes.*

Always preoccupied by the weather of the day, these islanders use the least statement on the matter as the occasion for a verbal joust.

The writer Patrick Sugrue describes in these few lines the very essence of life in the Blaskets:

The reader must imagine that small, lonely island, the most western habitation in Europe, cut off from the life and knowledge of Europe. Of God's gifts what they have must be snatched through toil and constant peril from the mouth of sea and storm. He must imagine men and women reared in hardship and aware of the constant threat of poverty and hunger hanging over them. A little satisfies them and, when that little comes their way, they are lively, cheerful, jesting people.... To them Ireland is a distant country. Springfield or Holyoke, Mass, is more of a capital city for them than any in their land of their birth. They have no newspapers, no library, no secondary school, only the learning that comes naturally to them, and which stamps their minds, from the constant intercourse with nature, with the pitiless beauty of the world, with the wildness and calm and wind and sea....

After the First World War, the island started its decline. The young were no longer prepared to accept the rigours of their lives and their isolation. The faraway cities attracted them. Their parents remained faithful to the island to the end. However, by 1930, there was no more turf and, in 1947, only fifty people remained and the school was closed. In 1953 the island was finally abandoned by its last twenty inhabitants. Tomás O'Crohan himself wrote the epitaph for his tombstone: 'Our like will never be seen again.'

Nowadays only three people live on the island in the summertime. Sue Redican, a weaver, sells her work in the little cottage that she has renovated. A German woman, Eta Bode, and her companion Anne Kavanagh, run a café and a youth hostel for an Irish company that has bought back two-thirds of the island from an American. Several boats leave Dingle or Dunquin bringing tourists and bird-watchers.... Grass has grown over the once well-trodden paths. Most of the houses are abandoned, though some are less dilapidated than others.

The last survivor lives at Dunquin. Seated beside the fire in a bare kitchen, he tirelessly looks out of the window at the light playing on the 5 kilometres (3 miles) of ocean that separate him from his island. Speaking in Gaelic, his only language, he chats with his friend, the schoolmaster, in Dunquin. He tells me that his body may be living in Dunquin, but he has never left his island.

ABOVE *We sail along Inis Beg's rocks. Wild Inishtearaght can be seen in the background.*

LEFT *Dunleavy house and the ruins of a beehive hut.*

PAGES 116 AND 117 *We are travelling north to south and drop anchor at the first island of the Blasket archipelago. It is called Beginish (meaning 'small island'). Sheep love its sweet grass.*

ABOVE, RIGHT
*Sue Redican is a weaver who
lives in the Blaskets during
the summer.*

ABOVE *Dunquin, Slea Head, Beginish and the ruins of the village.*

RIGHT *This bell was used in the film* Ryan's Daughter *when it was shot in 1969. I don't know how it found its way to the island. I prefer to believe it is an Easter bell that was lost on its way back from Rome.*

Inishtearaght seen above the rocks near Slea Head.

These donkeys are the only full-time residents of Great Blasket. Here they are nibbling grass alongside the gable belonging to Maurice O' Sullivan, famous for his book Twenty Years A-Growing.

RIGHT *The path leading to the harbour is overgrown with weeds.*

BELOW *Calm and serenity descend upon you when you see Clogher Head and a little fishing boat on a balmy summer evening.... If you come back in December, you'll feel you have landed on another planet.*

SKELLIGS ISLANDS

The islands of the

The two islands of the Skelligs resemble two great pyramids of granite. They appear and disappear, dramatic and mysterious, in the mists of the Atlantic horizon off St Finian's Bay in Co. Kerry. The monastery on Skellig Michael (Great Skellig), the larger of the two, was founded in the sixth century when Christianity first appeared in Ireland. It is known that the monastery was later attacked several times by the Vikings, who condemned Abbot Eitgal to death by leaving him to die of hunger on a rock.

There are very few records about the monks' way of life on the island, but evidently they had to descend 670 steps in the morning in order to fish for their breakfast, before ascending them again to devote their days to prayer and the study of religion, in the little round monastic cells that can be seen to this day. The monastery was finally abandoned in the thirteenth century.

However, a couple of years later it had become one of the most famous places of pilgrimage in Europe. There are plenty of tales and legends about these pilgrimages, and evidently with the passing of the years the pilgrims became less and less ascetic.... At the end of the eighteenth century, there were only young pilgrims of both sexes who got together there to dance and enjoy themselves far from the eyes of their elders. The ribald activities have been well documented in defamatory humorous poems known as the 'Skelligs List'.

Gannets can live for at least twenty years and will always come back to the very rock where they were hatched. What is more, they choose a partner for life.

The smaller of the two islands, Little Skellig, is an incredible place to study and observe seabirds. It has the largest colony of gannets in the west of Ireland.

I came sailing from the Blaskets one fine morning with Joe. Fine morning? Not exactly! The Blaskets suddenly appeared before us when the northwest wind finally came and chased away the clouds that veiled them. However, the sea was too rough to allow us to go alongside at Skellig Michael. We spent three astonishing hours a few cables from Little Skellig, admiring the incessant ballet of 30,000 pairs of gannets. The noise was deafening and the smell of tons of guano did not encourage us to cook the turbots that a fisherman friend had given us.

Gannets can live for at least twenty years and will always come back to the very rock where they were hatched. What is more they choose a

The lighthouse of Skellig Michael nestles amongst the highest rocks.

partner for life. They will be breeding from the age of five or six, one single egg being laid at a time. According to scientific research, ninety per cent of them will take flight. Then the most crucial period follows. The young ones simply throw themselves into the sea, knowing little or nothing about flying. They suddenly find themselves without parents to teach them and have to learn to feed themselves by instinct. At this stage they are heavier than their parents and too fat to fly. They have sufficient reserves of fat to survive for a week without eating. Then, slimmed down, they begin to fly and to find their own food.

The young ones are great travellers. In winter they may be found in the Mediterranean and even off tropical Africa. With age, the birds tend to travel less; they content themselves with little winter jaunts. Gannets eat fish, such as garfish and mackerel, to a maximum length of 30 centimetres ($11\frac{1}{2}$ inches). To catch them, they do not hesitate to make vertiginous dives, straight down into the water at high speed. The young ones take their first big plunge into the nourishing waters in mid-August.

Gannets stay on the Skellig Islands till the month of September, so the summer is the ideal period to observe them. Day trips are organized all summer long from Port Magee, the nearest port, on the sound facing Valentia Island. You need good weather to be able to land, but an ornithologist spends much of the summer there studying the gannets and acting as a guide for the visitors.

ABOVE *A small section of the colony of gannets settled on a large area of guano.*

RIGHT *Unhappily for us, the wind is picking up to force 6 to 7 and we cannot land on Skellig Michael.*

PAGES 124 AND 125 *Thousands of gannets come every year to Little Skellig to breed and spend their summer. It is Ireland's largest seabird, with a wingspan of 2 metres (over 6 feet). Its is estimated that 30,000 pairs form this colony.*

The whole island is alive with gannets. Every square of the serrated cliffs has been claimed and decorated in a bright guano lime wash.

ABOVE *The Skelligs appear and disappear in a morning mist that is lifting very slowly.*

LEFT *The warden's hut.*

ABOVE *The last cloud unrolls itself like a white stoat wrap and unveils the summit for an instant.*

LEFT *The next day, on our way south, the weather settles and the wind dies down.*

DURSEY ISLAND
The island of the cable car

The Beara Peninsula, between Kenmare River and Bantry Bay, is the western end of Co. Cork and the southwestern point of Ireland. The proximity of the Gulf Stream, which brings warm water from the Gulf of Mexico, gives it a kinder climate and more luxuriant vegetation than is to be found further up the coast. At its western extremity is Dursey Island and on its southern flank, Bere Island.

Incidentally, oceanographers assert that the Gulf Stream has already lost twenty per cent of its volume in the last decade, and is seriously at risk owing to the effects of global warming and the melting of the Arctic ice cap.

Dursey, the lonely western extremity, is of all the inhabited islands, the most tranquil. It has no café, no restaurant, no hotel and no guest house. At 6.5 kilometres (4 miles) long, 1.5 kilometres (nearly 1 mile) wide, it is a paradise for walkers and bird-watchers.

It was not always a paradise, as it was on Dursey that the Vikings used to keep their Irish slaves, while waiting for boats to take them to Scandinavia. The forces of Elizabeth I were crueller still – when they invaded the island in 1601, they pushed all the Irish men, women and children into the Atlantic from the top of the highest cliffs.

Nowadays you make the passage from the mainland to the island in a cable car suspended 26 metres (85 feet) above the waves in six minutes. The only Irish cable car, it can transport six people, ten sheep or one cow.

Sparsely populated, the Beara Peninsula is one of the jewels of southwestern Ireland.

It's a funny kind of experience to be suspended over the Atlantic in the little blue cab, sitting on a hard wooden bench, with the dung of... sheep sticking to your feet.

It's a funny kind of experience to be suspended over the Atlantic in the little blue cab, sitting on a hard wooden bench, with the dung of the last passengers (sheep) sticking to your feet. The machine does not look very solid, but, if it can transport a dairy cow, I reckon I have a pretty good chance of getting to the other side in one piece. Even with big winds, there has never been an accident.

Safely delivered to the island, I am in a different world. The only little road winds between the ruins of the three villages overhanging the sea. Hundreds of birds wheel in the updraughts of the cliffs, now, though level with me, 150 metres (492 feet) above the waves, now squawking just above my head.

Paying attention neither to me nor to the precipice beside them, sheep quietly graze the tender grass on the cliff tops. I stop a moment to photograph a dog and a cat, lying cuddled together in the sunshine. They are the companions of Jimmy Walsh, one of the seven residents of the island. Introducing myself, I ask him if I can take a few photos. He makes no objection and gives me a timid little smile. He has the copper complexion of people who live in the open air. Stretched out on the grass, we build a simple friendship in the course of a meandering conversation…. We speak of everything and nothing and, in this place, it doesn't matter much, there is plenty of time…. He lives in a bare house, and he tells me that he has all he needs and does not feel much desire to go 'ashore'. 'From time to time, when I feel like it,' he says calmly.

With my camera-bag on my back, I walk around the island, which takes me all afternoon. On my return past Jimmy's house, I can hear the commentary on a football match that is taking place in…Italy. This sound gives me a surreal sensation. It is five o'clock in the afternoon, and already today I have driven 100 kilometres (62 miles) by car, passed through towns and villages, taken a cable car and dozens of photos, walked 10 kilometres (6 miles) and now here I am preparing to leave again…. By contrast, Jimmy has not left his house, and is drinking a cup of tea while he watches twenty-two men chase a bag of wind in…Italy.

The load on my back tells me that, of the two of us, it's certainly Jimmy who has the right idea.

With your shoes resting on sheep's droppings, your bottom sitting on a hard wooden bench, you are suspended above the Atlantic in this small blue car. You have six minutes to strike up a conversation if your travelling companion is two-legged.

ABOVE At this spot you are 3,310 kilometres (2,057 miles) from Moscow.

PAGES 132 AND 133 It takes six minutes in the cable car, 100 metres (328 feet) above the sea, to bring you from the mainland to Dursey.

To your right, the Skelligs. To your left, and below, the sea. Above, the sky. Six long minutes ahead, Dursey.

Cottage to let, 50 metres above the sea.

The Bull Island lighthouse lies to the northwest of Dursey.

LEFT AND ABOVE *Jimmy has the rugged face of the outdoor man. His eyes, like his house and his life, are uncluttered. He is happy with his lot.*

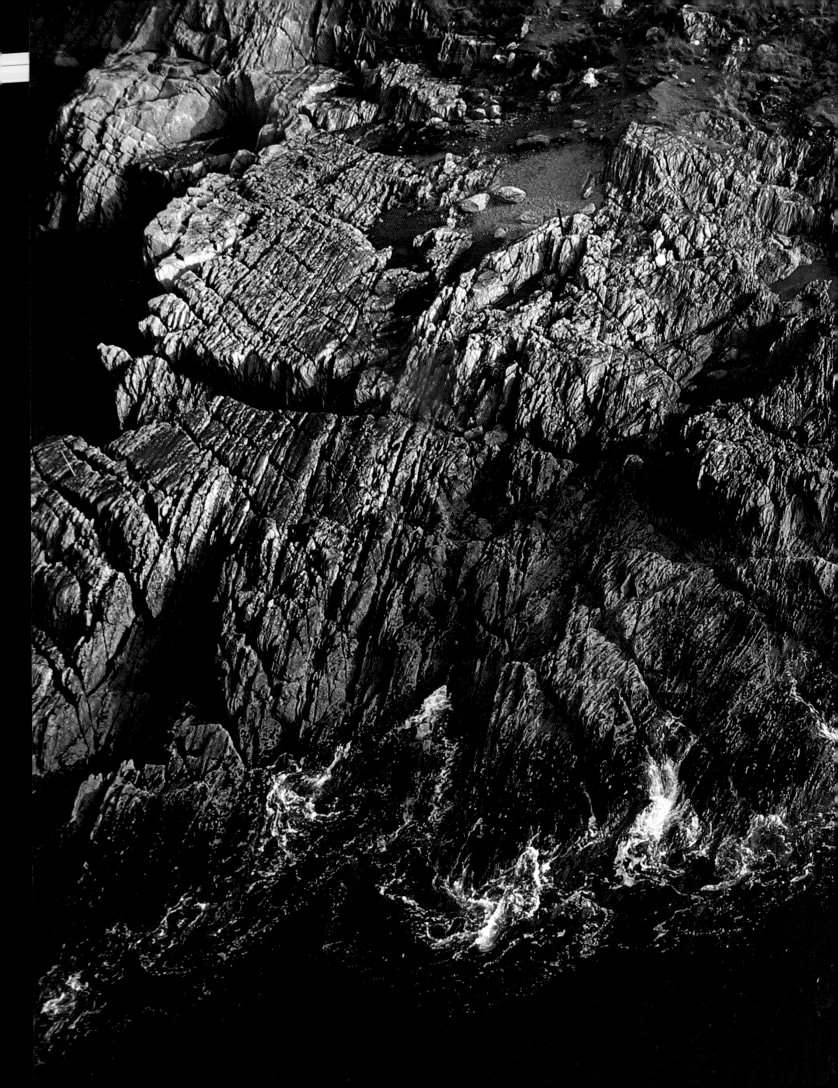

An old worn-out punt acts as a roof for a fisherman's shed.

TOP *Scarlet fuchsias and waterfall. Everything here is natural.*

PAGES 138 AND 139 *The sea is quiet to day. From a hole in the cable car's floor, I have a bird's-eye view over the waves and the rocks below.*

ABOVE *Dursey is 6 kilometres (over 3½ miles) long and a paradise for ramblers and bird-watchers. Of all the islands I have visited, it is the quietest.*

The sun is setting over Dursey and the Beara Peninsula.

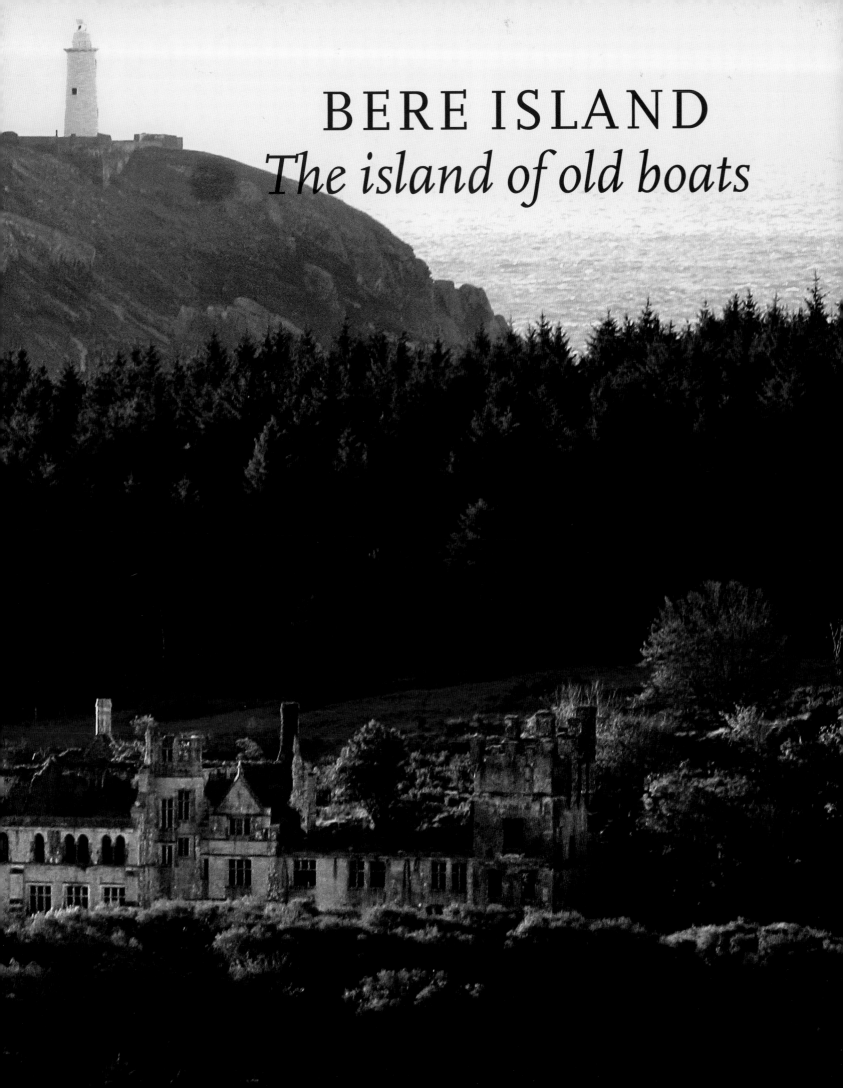

BERE ISLAND
The island of old boats

Bere Island, a five-minute ferry ride from Castletownbere, still belonged to Britain until 1938, even though Ireland had become independent in 1921.

In 1796 a fierce battle was fought off the island, in which the Irish hero Wolfe Tone and General Hinoche, third officer to Napoleon Bonaparte, took on the English fleet. It was a disaster for the French and the Irish. After their victory, the English decided to fortify the harbour of Berehaven against any future attacks from the sea, building many fortifications. This British base played a vital role during the First World War, providing a base from which the Royal Navy and the Americans could control this part of the Atlantic.... Today, life is a lot more peaceful here in what has become a little corner of paradise.

As the port of Castletownbere provides employment for many people, and access to the island is so easy – a five-minute ride in one of the two ferries that make the crossing – the population is stable. There are a several retired people and holiday homes there, while the Irish army uses part of the island as a training camp.

Walking round the island, I came to a little bay that serves as a cemetery for about ten old boats. I was sad to discover among the wrecks an old classic from Galway Bay on which I had slaved for three years; a púcán (a small hooker, a traditional sailing boat). I had knocked her into shape and sold her to a Scottish fisherman.

My old friend was in a wretched state and while I was taking a few photos, with a tear in my eye, a lady came up and addressed me: 'Does that boat interest you?' she asked. I explained to her that the boat had once belonged to me and spoke lovingly of it. We both agreed that it was very sad to see a boat that has been let go. She invited me to come and have a cup of tea in her house nearby.

Sarah and Noel Muckley had left England to live on Bere Island a few years ago. They came with the idea of starting a school of traditional boat building. Noel built his workshop beside the water and started repairing old wooden boats – a labour of love that hardly gave them enough to live on. Everybody wants fibreglass or aluminium: wood is not valued any more.

The Scottish fisherman and his wife separated, and that lady gave the púcán to Noel for repair. She hopes to sell her to an enthusiast for old-fashioned boats. Noel loves his work and I spent two very agreeable hours watching him at it. He has the smell of sawdust in his blood, he tells me. He handles the plane like a paintbrush, and with his agile fingers, his pleasure is to bring the gracious curves of the past back to life. My old boat is in good hands.

Noel Muckley's workshop.

PAGES 142 AND 143 *If you climb the hills, west of Castletownbere, you will have a good view of Ardnakinna Point, the western point of Bere. Hidden in the wood, on the mainland, are the ruins of the mansion belonging to the Puxleys. This Anglo-Irish family made a fortune running and developing the copper mines in the area. The house was set ablaze by the old IRA in 1921.*

'Does that boat interest you?' she asked. I explained to her that the boat had once belonged to me and spoke lovingly of her.

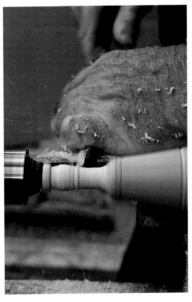

Noel Muxley worked all his life as a shipwright in England. He spends his time on the island giving new life to old wooden boats.

ABOVE *A rare sight: a derelict cottage. New houses outnumber the derelict ones on Bere Island.*

RIGHT *An old boat's graveyard.*

Hungry Hill, facing Bere Island in the Beara Peninsula, is aptly named.

May the music of the sea be like a choir of angels to you

On board the *Anna M*, at the pleasure of the winds, I went to discover what was, what is and what in the near future will be the life of the islands. I was only a visitor, however, and I would like to pass the word to Mary Sugrue, daughter of the last inhabitant of Horse Island, near Ballinskelligs in Co. Kerry.

She wrote for me in Gaelic, straight from her experience, and she exposes, in a few paragraphs, the reality that was life on the islands of Ireland.

It was on a small island called the Island of the Horses that I was born on the 8th of February 1942. My father was a fisherman, Padraig MacGearailt, like my grandfather. My mother was from Imeallach na Muc on the Coireáin road, Bríghid Nic Chártaigh. There was one person older than me and that was a brother who died shortly after arriving in the world. I have two other brothers and two sisters living and it was on the Island that the four of us were born.

Maidhcí Leidhin, who lived in Ring, was telling me that he was making some lazy beds in the garden on the 9th of February 1942, the day after my birthday, when my father came looking for him to bring his family with his horse and cart to the chapel to baptise me.

According to Maidhcí, my head was wetted with stuff that was much stronger than holy water as the men developed a taste for the drink on the way back to the boat and when they were well on they took the infant, myself, in the boat with them. It was probably a miracle of God that I survived my first boat journey on the sea that day.

I remember that when my mother was about to give birth to my sister, Eibhlín, that my father went out in the boat to the nurse. When they weren't coming, my people at home became anxious and my grandfather lit a fire outside the house on the Island to get them to hurry up. But, alas, it was a waste because the child was born half an hour before the nurse landed at the port on the Island. God help anyone on the Island in those days who was depending on getting a nurse or a doctor urgently.

Life on the Island was always hard and when we grew up we had to learn about everything to do with boats: how to put it in the water and how to row and how to pull it on the strand.

One other family, the de Barra's, were with us on the island but they left and we spend almost six years on our own with no one that might help us.

When the sea would be quiet, we would row to school, as it was usual for my father to be away fishing. My mother would be watching us from the house until we had reached the harbour out there and again in the afternoon. she would not take her eyes off us until we were safely on the Island strand. There was a lot of anxiety involved in the life of the Island that no one would understand but a mother who raised her family there.

I was always afraid of the journey from school on Fridays because on that day it was my grandfather who used to be in charge of the boat after getting his pension and he would have quiet a lot of porter on board. He was a man who would become very unafraid, hopeful altogether on the sea when the drink would be giving him extra courage and instead of going in nice and steady with the flow, he would make for the big, threatening waves out in Bealach, his cap flying so that, we, the children, were frightened out of our lives.

If the weather were rough we would have to stay at home from school. During the winter we would always have extra groceries in the house in case a long period of bad weather would come and, more important than that, extra tobacco because if there should be a shortage of tobacco no one could put up with the men in our house.

Many storms hit the Island of the Horses in my youth, but there was one particular one which will live in my memory forever. St Stephen's night in the year of 1951, it was. The morning was lovely and calm and my parents had arranged to go to visit my aunt on the mainland. My grandfather was to go with them, but when they were just ready to leave my father said he did not like the sky in the west. He was a man who had a great ability to read the signs of the weather. My grandfather left but my parents stayed. By my soul, it was a good thing for us that they stayed as that night the storm blew worse that it ever hit the island in my memory.

Not only that but there flashes of lightning and rolls of thunder exploding and the disturbed sea rising beyond. The waves rose above the cliffs at the back of the Island and the flood came flowing down over the fields.

I remember that we were all pent up in my parent's bedroom downstairs together after we had fled from the upper rooms when the wind broke into us through the roof. My mother was sprinkling holy water into every part and my father walking in an anxious way between the hearth and the dresser. That night left me afraid of storms from then on.

It was from Ceanúg on the mainland that the turf came to the Island. The day that the turf was being cut we would light a fire in the bog to make the tea for the men. The kettle and other things would have been taken by us from home. It was a fine, healthy meal; brown bread and boiled eggs. Then, when the turf would be saved and dry we would take it to the harbour in Rinn with a white horse and cart that Mícheál the master would give us. We would make a stack of it at the edge of the sea and every trip we tool to the mainland after that we would take some bags of turf home with us in the boat until we had all on the Island.

There would always be a big fuss involved in bringing a cow to the market. We would have to put her swimming out behind the boat. The men would back the boat in at the edge of the strand. My father would jump into the boat then, holding the rope that would be tied to the cow's head. The work we would have to do as children was to threaten the cow into the water and, I am telling you, that was hard to do, it would take a long time before it would do anything for us. But as soon as we had her in the water, my father would row like a man in a hurry to keep the rope tight. There would be another journey of ten miles going to the market in Caherciveen, and they often be walking.

Christmas was always very enjoyable on the Island. My parents and the de Barra family would go to the mainland to Confession and to bring sweet things back with them. After they would return, we would have the traditional dinner for Christmas Eve, salted fish, white sauce and potatoes as it was a day of fasting. The custom at the time was that the youngest person and the oldest one would light the candles that would be stuck in jars of sand on the windows. Later in the night we would have Nash's lemonade and the men would have porter. Treacle bread, jam and Christmas cake was what we had for supper. After the rosary was said, my parents would go visiting to the de Barra's. Then, at a quarter to eleven we would go rowing to midnight mass in Dún Géagáin. It would be two o' clock in the morning before we would reach the house.

We would always be hoping for visits from our relatives. On occasions like that my father would play the box and there on the cement floor of my house on the Island I learnt my first waltz and the South Kerry set.

My father and uncle were fine sean-nós singers and so we would often have our own entertainment.

My grandfather died on the 28th of January in the year 1955 at the age of 83. We held a traditional wake in the house, pipes, tobacco, plenty of food and a barrel of porter and boats were coming and going through the night.

The following day the coffin was taken in the boat to the outside harbour, the other boats rowing slowly behind. A sea funeral and the coffin and the rowing oars shining under the low winter sun.

In the year 1957 I myself left the Island to go to work in Óstán Uí Mháine at the age of 16. After a bad storm in the month of November in the year 1959 my whole family abandoned the Island and they came to live in one of the houses at the cable station where my mother still lives. In the month of January 1997, my father died. He was an islander and a man of the sea to the marrow and these words are written on the gravestone: " May the music of the sea be like a choir of angels for you".

Although I would never return to the misery that belonged to my native Island, all the same I miss it all the time.

A special thanks to Mary Sugrue.